PIANO • VOCAL • GUITAR

# John Lennon
# Power To The People
# The Hits

ISBN 978-1-61780-706-0

HAL•LEONARD®
CORPORATION
7777 W. BLUEMOUND RD. P.O. BOX 13819 MILWAUKEE, WI 53213

Visit Hal Leonard Online at
**www.halleonard.com**

# POWER TO THE PEOPLE

Words and Music by
JOHN LENNON

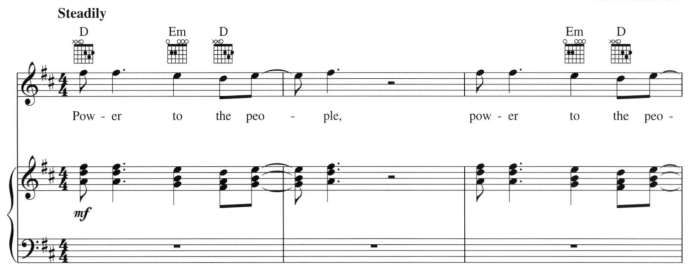

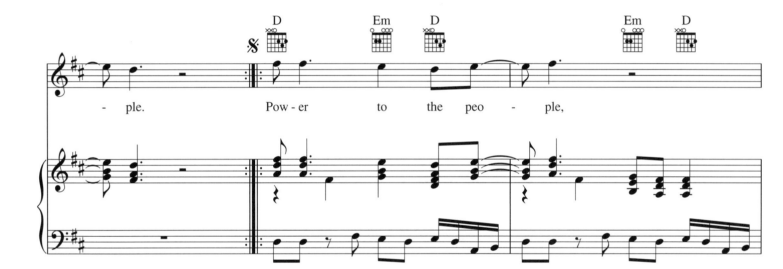

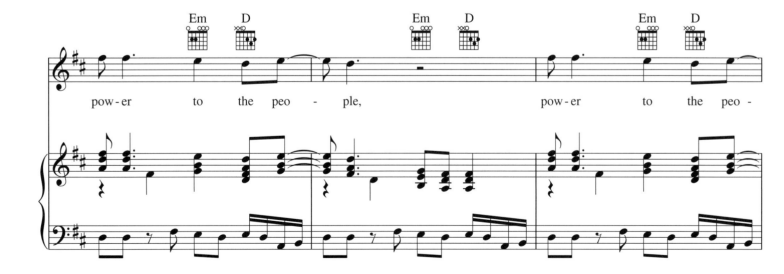

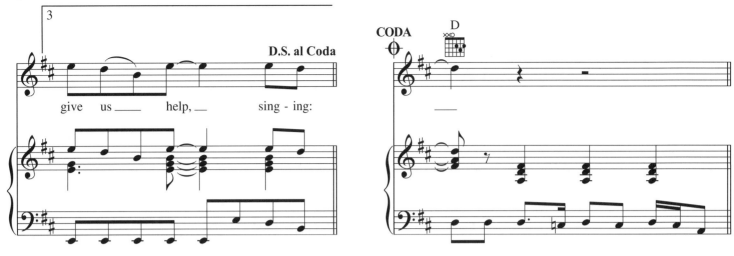

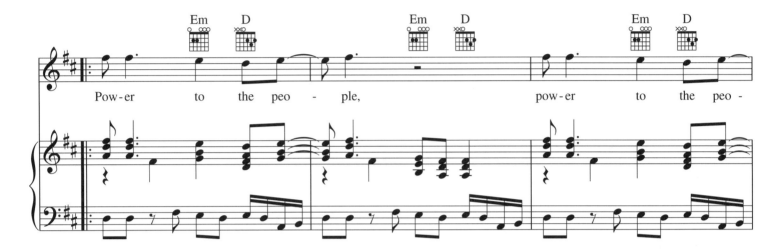

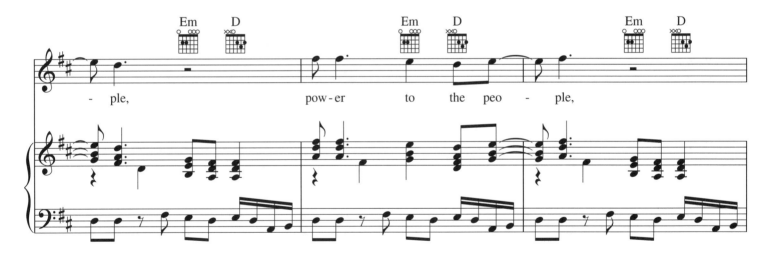

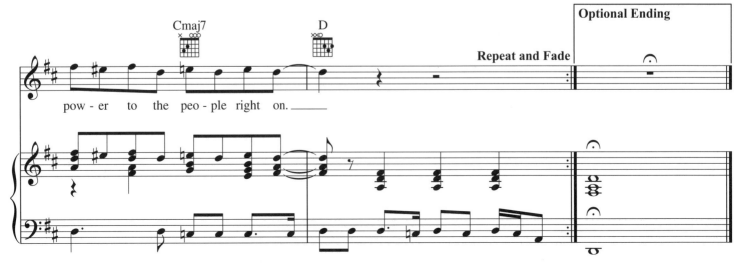

# GIMME SOME TRUTH

Words and Music by
JOHN LENNON

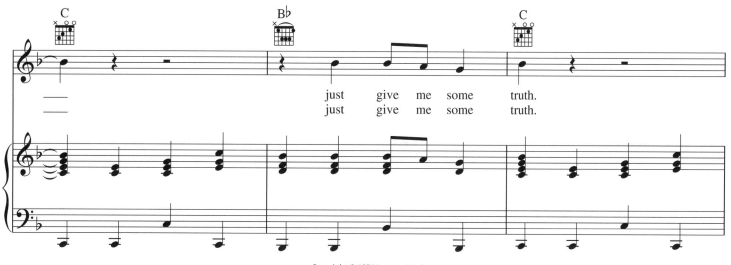

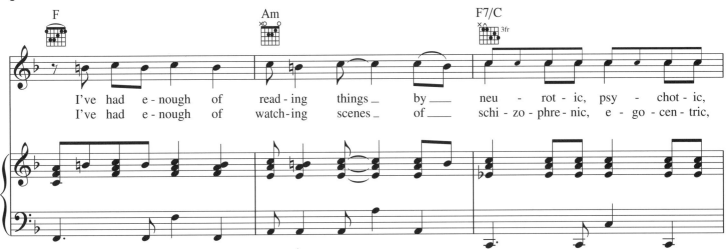

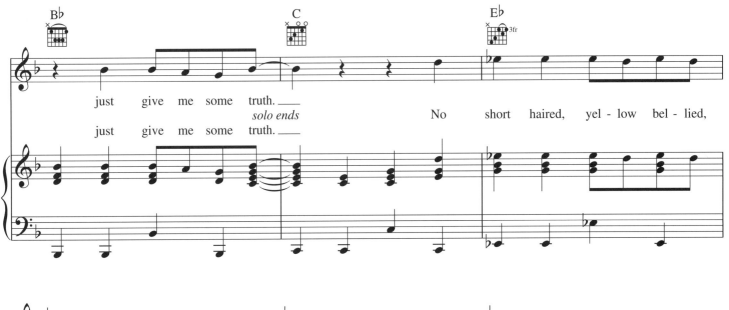

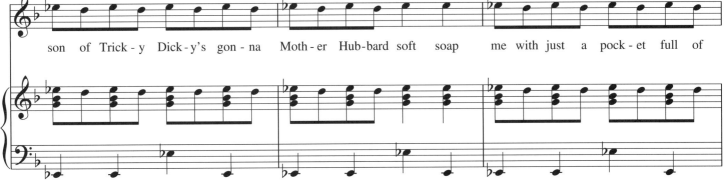

now.

Just give me some truth, ___ now.

I've had e - nough of read - ing things ___ by ___ neu - rot - ic, psy - chot - ic,

pig head - ed pol - i - ti - cians. All I want is the truth, ___ now.

**Repeat ad lib. and Fade**

**Optional Ending**

Just give me some truth, ___ now.

# WOMAN

Words and Music by
JOHN LENNON

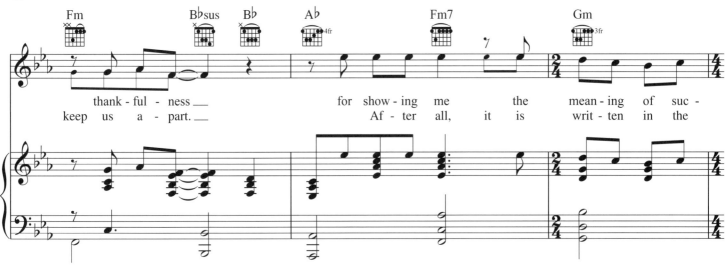

thank - ful - ness ___ for show - ing me the mean - ing of suc-
keep us a - part. ___ Af - ter all, it is writ - ten in the

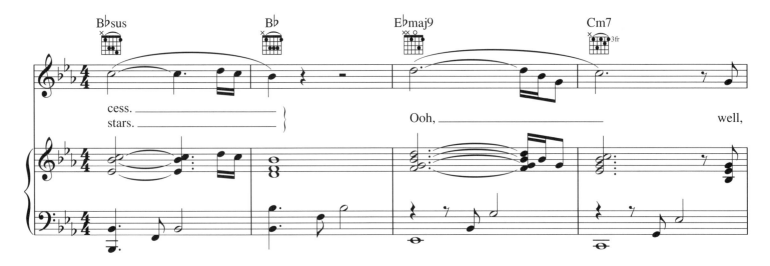

cess. ___
stars. ___
Ooh, ___ well,

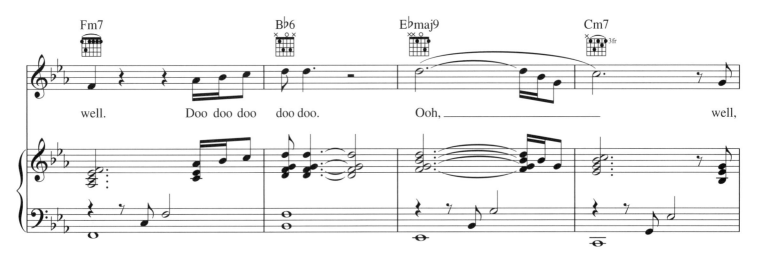

well. Doo doo doo doo doo. Ooh, ___ well,

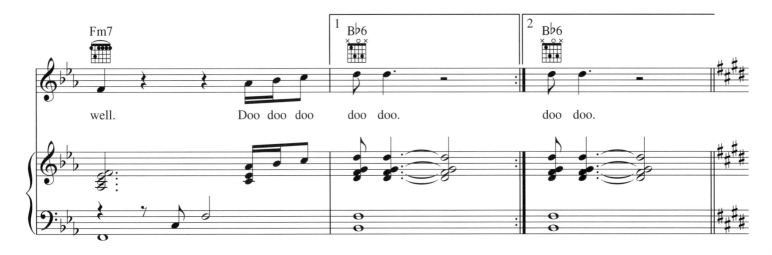

well. Doo doo doo doo doo. doo doo.

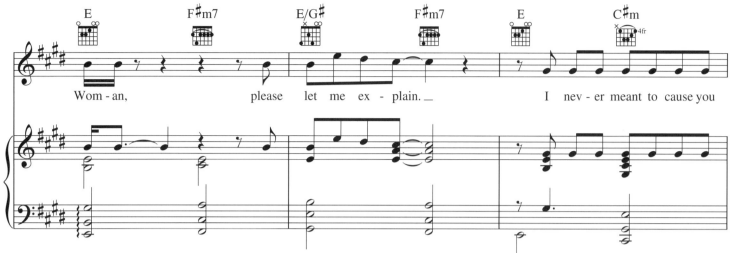

Wom-an, please let me ex-plain. _ I nev-er meant to cause you

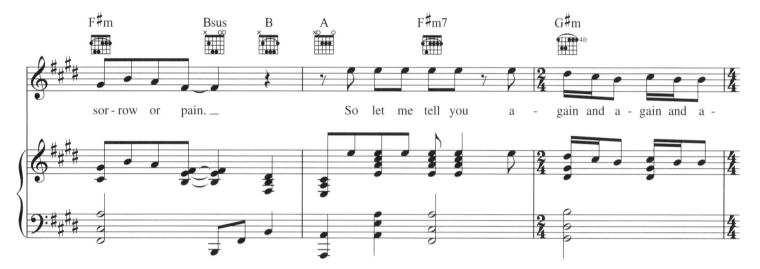

sor-row or pain. _ So let me tell you a - gain and a - gain and a -

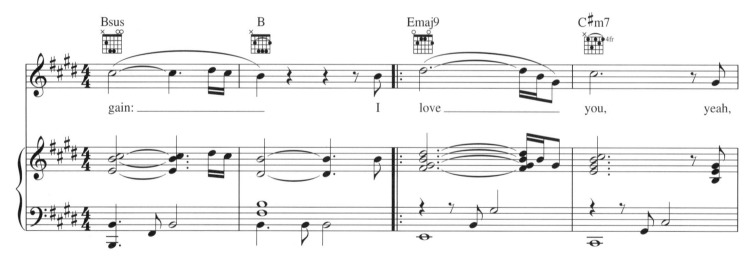

gain: _____ I love _____ you, yeah,

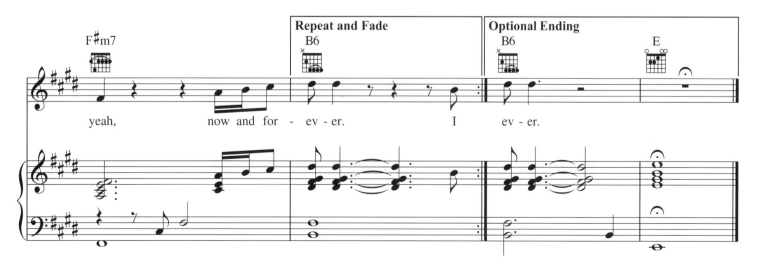

yeah, now and for - ev - er. I ev - er.

# INSTANT KARMA

Words and Music by
JOHN LENNON

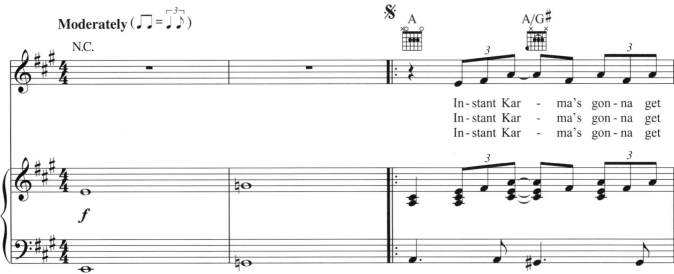

In-stant Kar - ma's gon-na get you,
In-stant Kar - ma's gon-na get you,
In-stant Kar - ma's gon-na get you,

gon - na knock you right __ on the head. __
gon - na look you right __ in the face. __
gon - na kock you off __ your feet. __

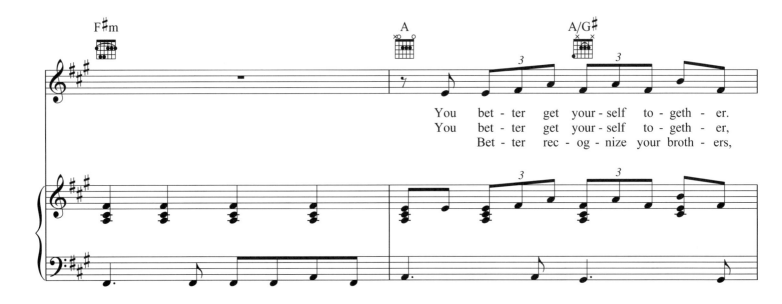

You bet - ter get your-self to-geth - er.
You bet - ter get your-self to-geth - er,
Bet - ter rec - og-nize your broth - ers,

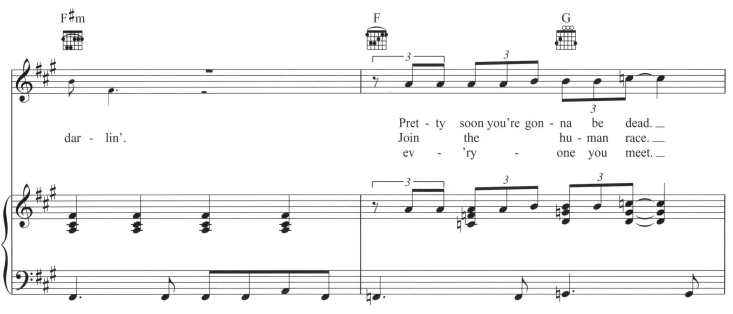

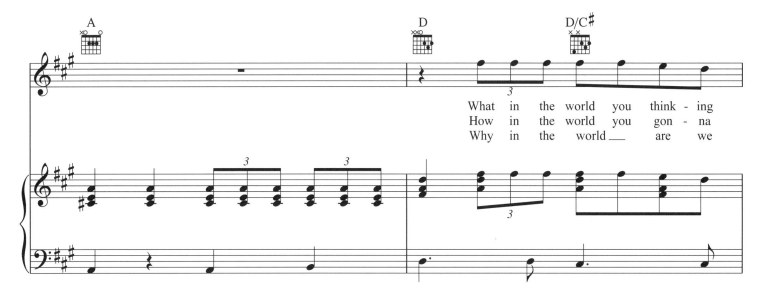

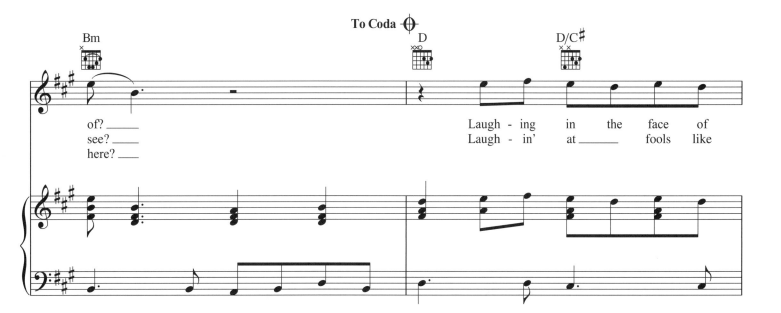

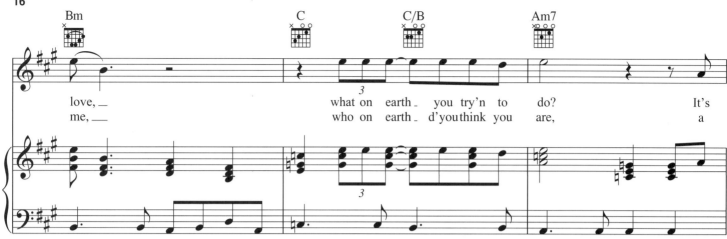

love, ___ what on earth ___ you try'n to do? It's
me, ___ who on earth ___ d'you think you are,  a

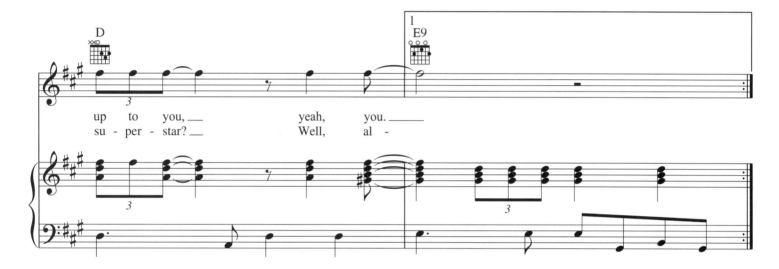

up to you, ___ yeah, you. _____
su - per - star? ___ Well, al -

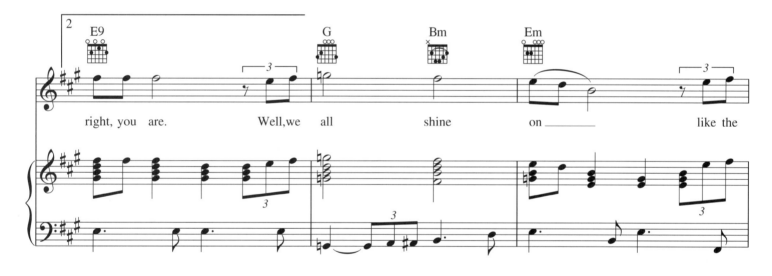

right, you are. Well, we all shine on _____ like the

moon ___ and the stars ___ and the sun. _____ Well, we all shine

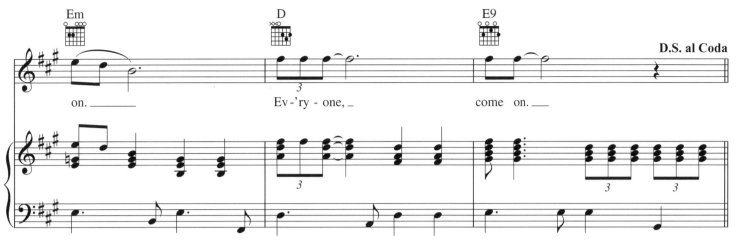

D.S. al Coda

on. _____ Ev-'ry - one, \_ come on. \_\_

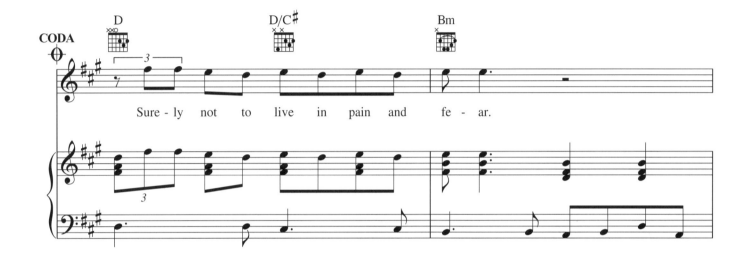

Sure - ly not to live in pain and fe - ar.

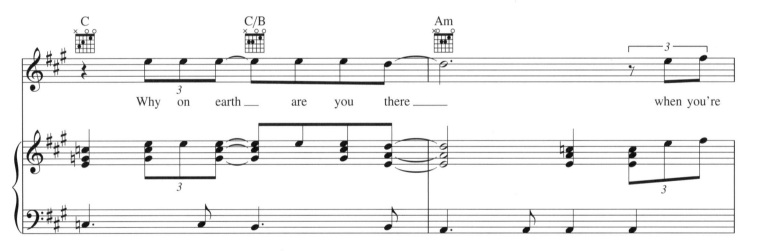

Why on earth \_\_ are you there \_\_\_\_\_ when you're

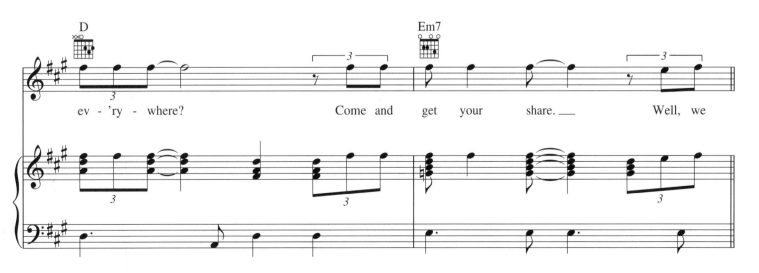

ev - 'ry - where? Come and get your share. \_\_ Well, we

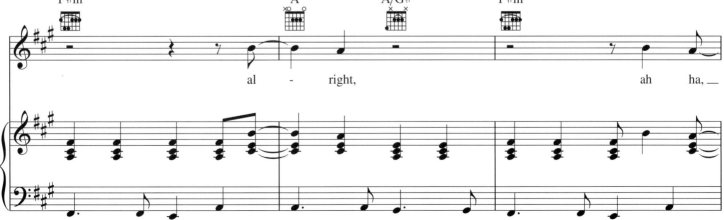

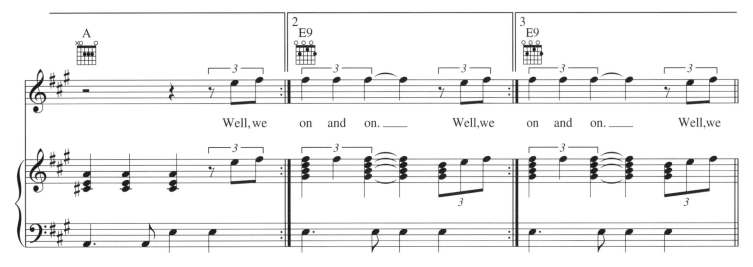

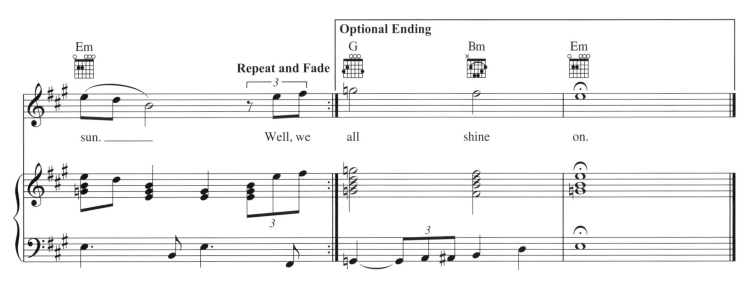

# WHATEVER GETS YOU THROUGH THE NIGHT

Words and Music by
JOHN LENNON

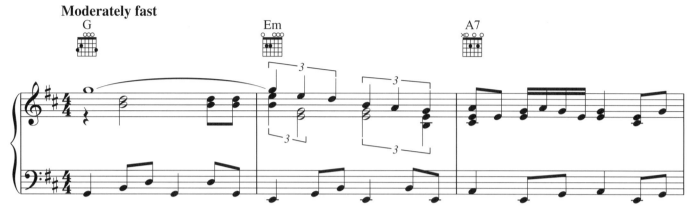

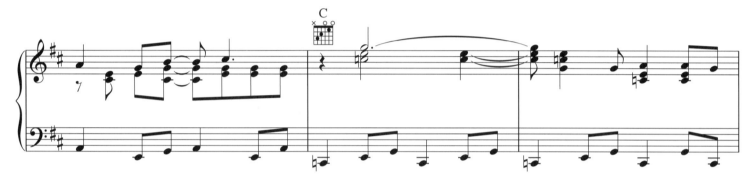

What-ev-er gets you through the

night 'sal - right, _ 'sal - right. _
life 'sal - right, _ 'sal - right. _
night 'sal - right, _ 'sal - right. _

It's your mon-ey or your life 'sal - right, _ 'sal -
Do it wrong or do it right 'sal - right, _ 'sal -
Out the blue or out of sight 'sal - right, _ 'sal -

- right. _ Don't need a gun to cut through flow - ers, _
- right. _ Don't need a watch to waste your time, _____
- right. _ Don't need a gun to blow your mind, _____

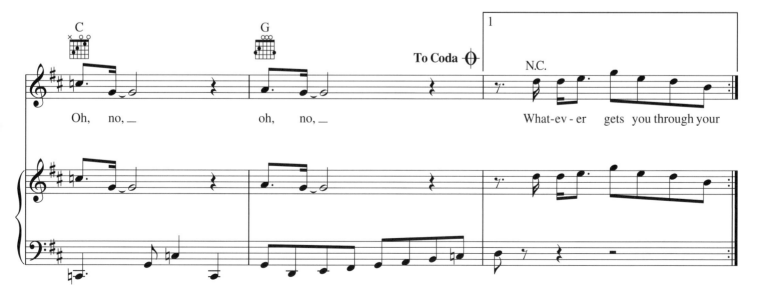

Oh, no, _ oh, no, _ What-ev - er gets you through your

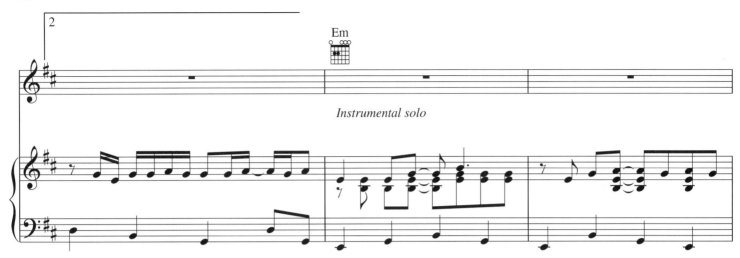

*Instrumental solo*

*Solo ends*

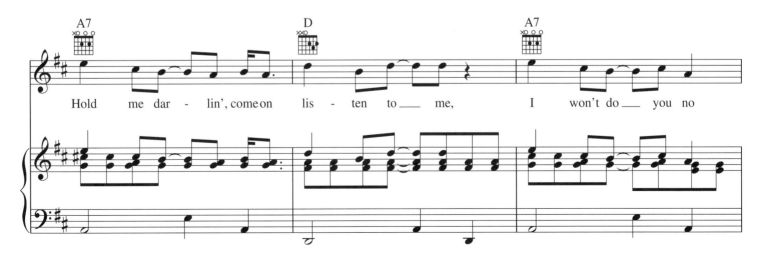

Hold me dar - lin', come on lis - ten to ___ me, I won't do ___ you no

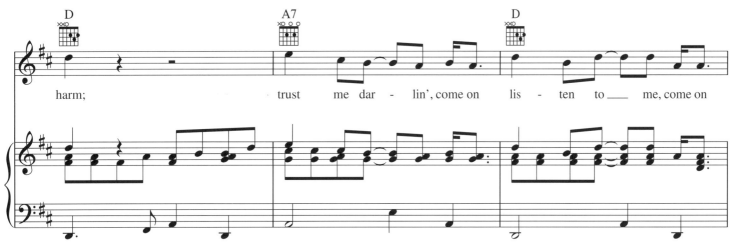

harm; trust me dar - lin', come on lis - ten to ___ me, come on

lis - ten to ___ me, come on lis - ten, ___ lis - ten. ___ *Instrumental solo*

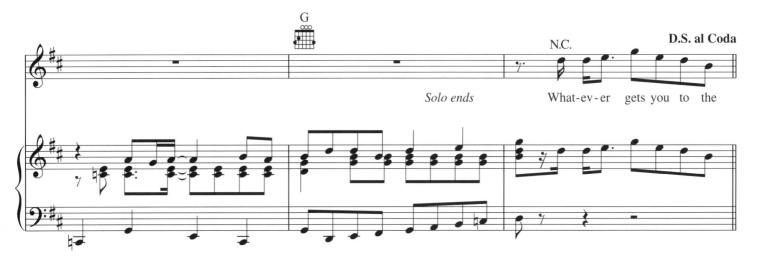

D.S. al Coda

N.C.

*Solo ends*     What-ev - er   gets you to the

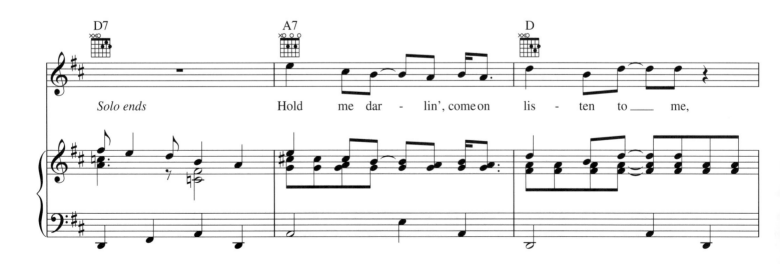

I won't do ___ you no harm; trust me dar - lin', come on

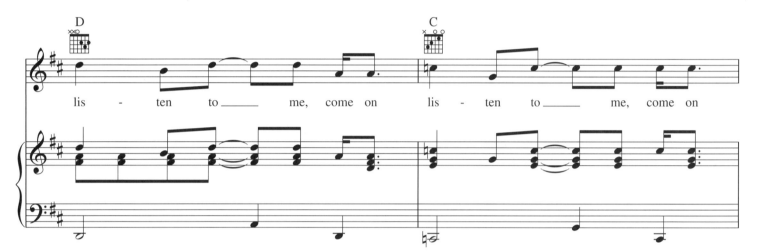

lis - ten to ___ me, come on lis - ten to ___ me, come on

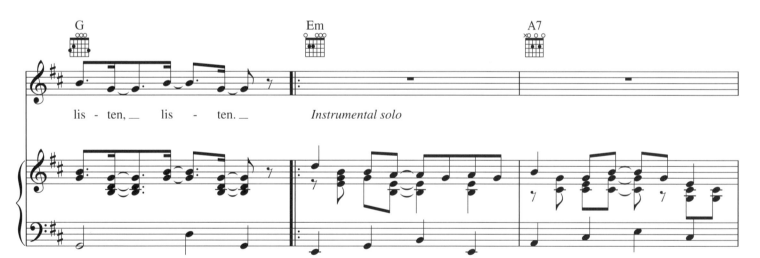

lis - ten, ___ lis - ten. ___ *Instrumental solo*

**Repeat and Fade**

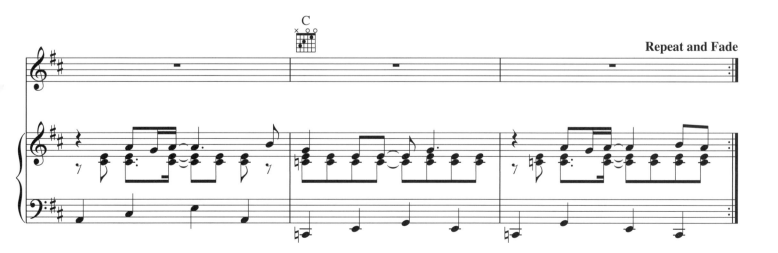

# COLD TURKEY

Words and Music by
JOHN LENNON

Tem - p'ra - ture's ris — ing
bod - y is ach — ing
Thir - ty - six hours _____

fe - ver is high _____
goose - pim - ple bone _____
roll - ing in pain _____

can't see no fu - ture
can't see no - bod - y
pray - ing to some - one

can't see no sky _____
leave me a - lone.
free me a - gain. _____

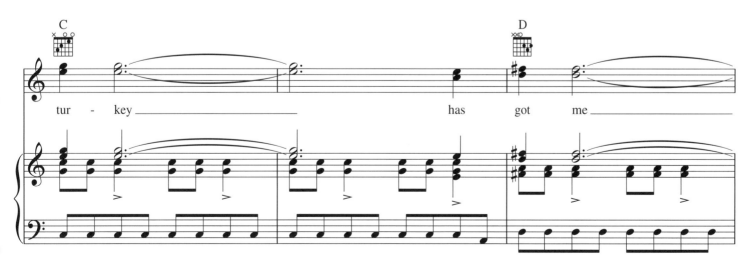

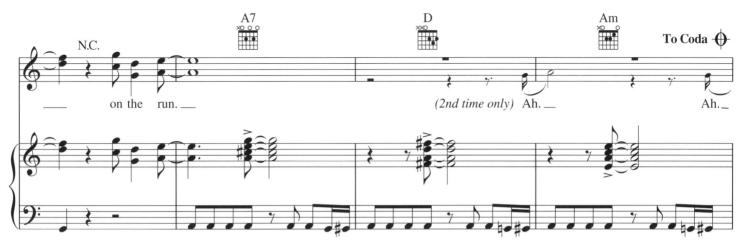

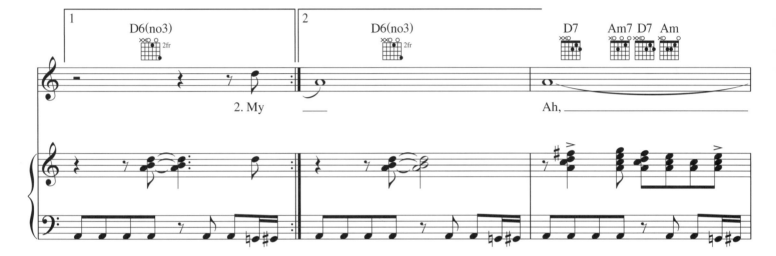

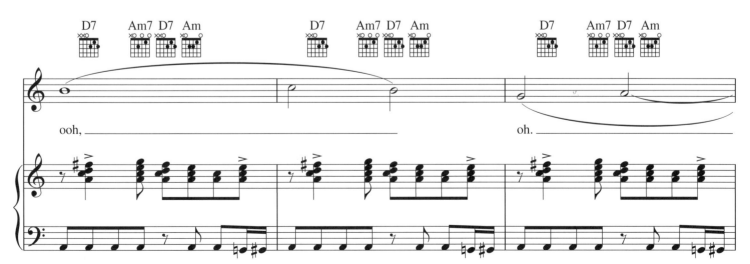

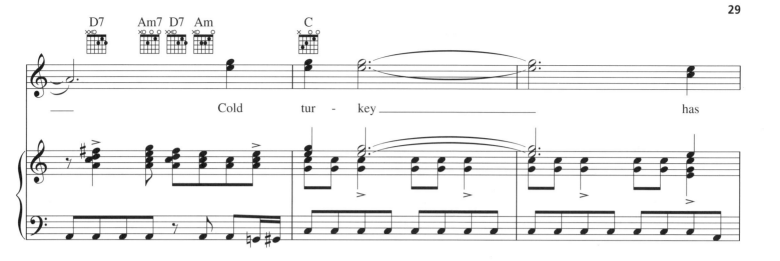

Cold tur - key _____ has

got me _____ on the run. ___ Oh, _

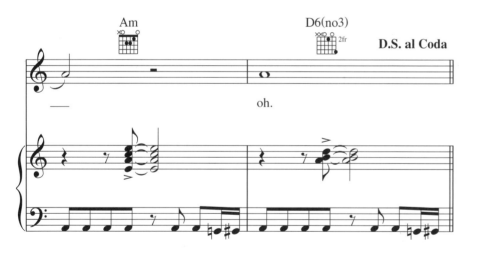

___ oh.

D.S. al Coda

**Repeat ad lib.**

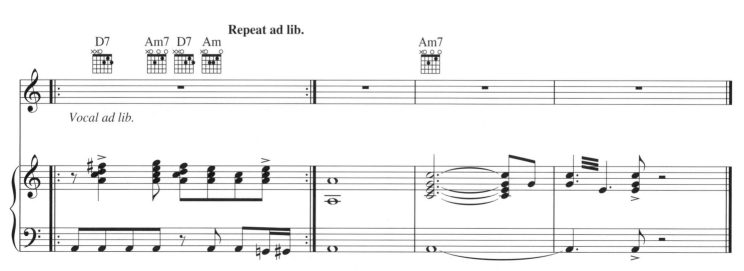

*Vocal ad lib.*

# JEALOUS GUY

Words and Music by
JOHN LENNON

**Easy Ballad**

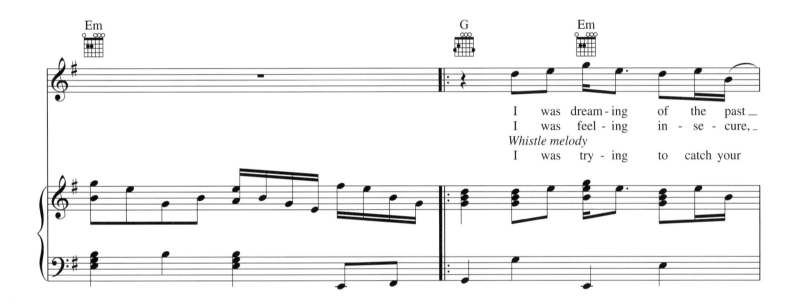

I was dream-ing of the past _
I was feel-ing in - se - cure, _
*Whistle melody*
I was try - ing to catch your

and my heart _ was beat - ing fast. _
you might not _ love me _ an - y -
thought that you _ was try - ing to hide. _

_ eyes,

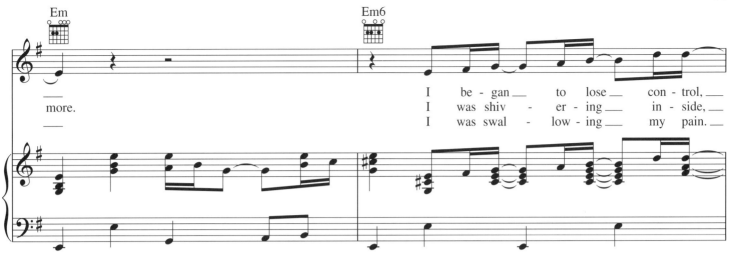

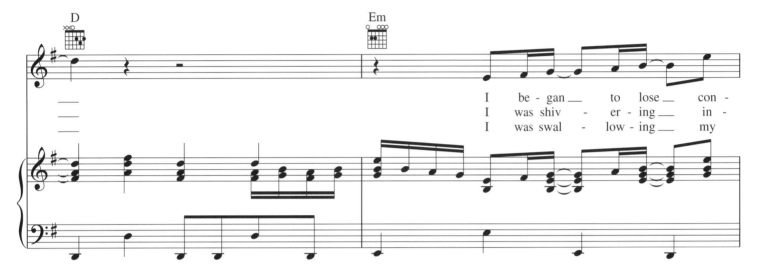

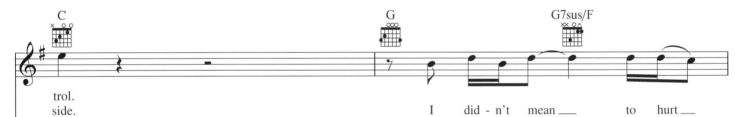

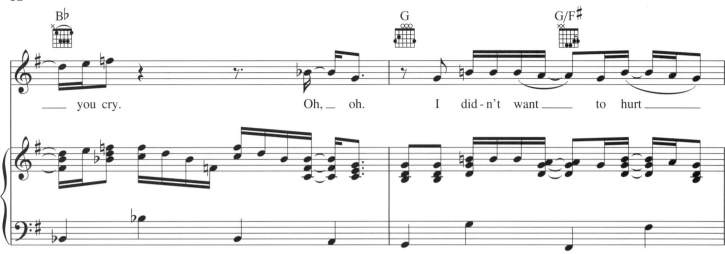

you cry. Oh,__ oh. I did-n't want__ to hurt__

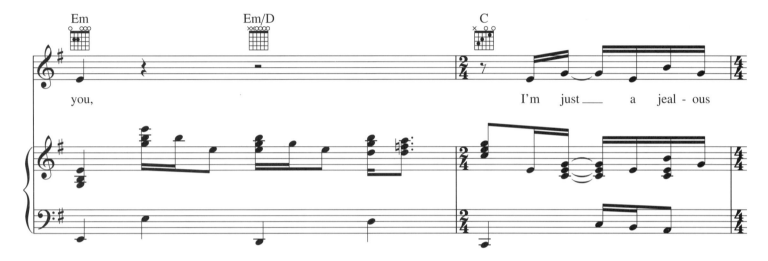

you, I'm just__ a jeal - ous

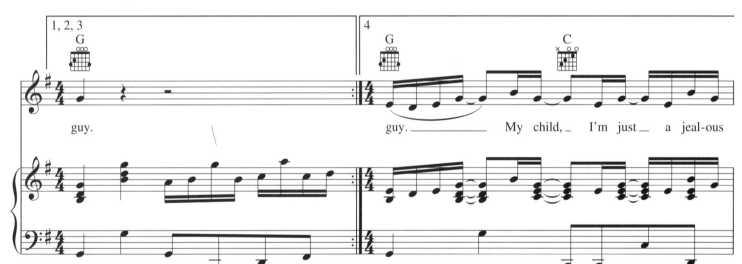

1, 2, 3

guy.

4

guy.__ My child,_ I'm just_ a jeal-ous

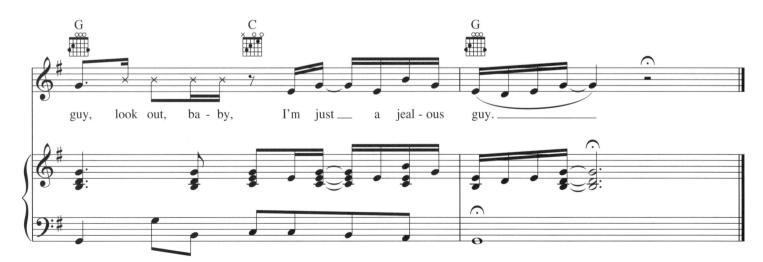

guy, look out, ba - by, I'm just__ a jeal - ous guy.__

# #9 DREAM

Words and Music by
JOHN LENNON

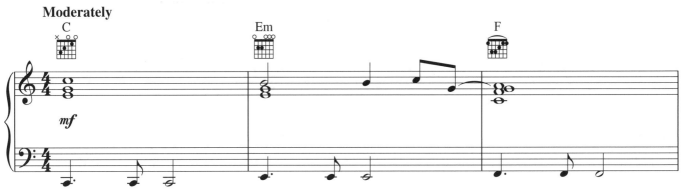

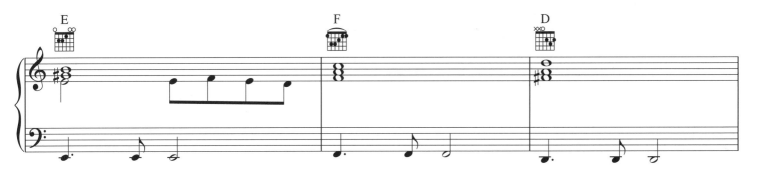

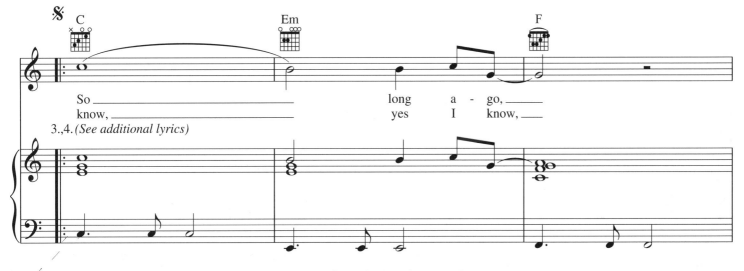

So _____ long a - go, _____
know, _____ yes I know, ____
3.,4. (See additional lyrics)

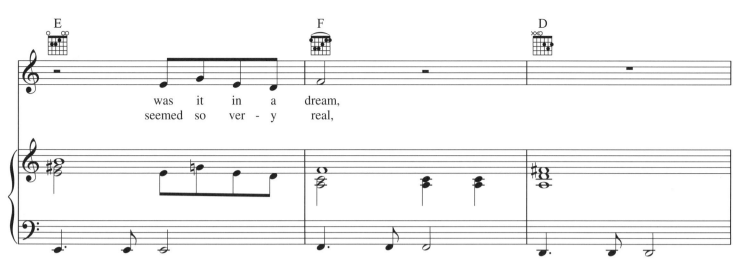

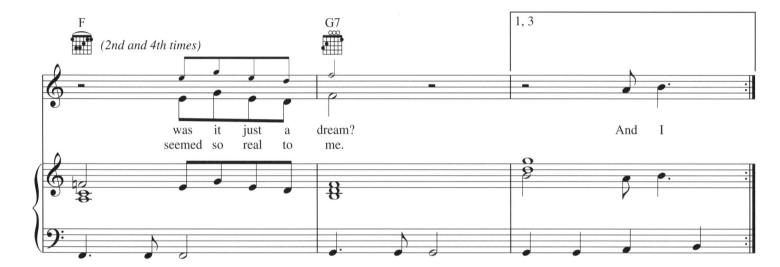

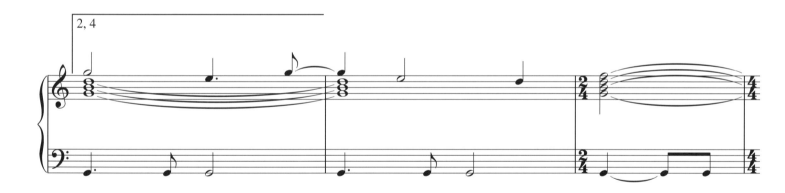

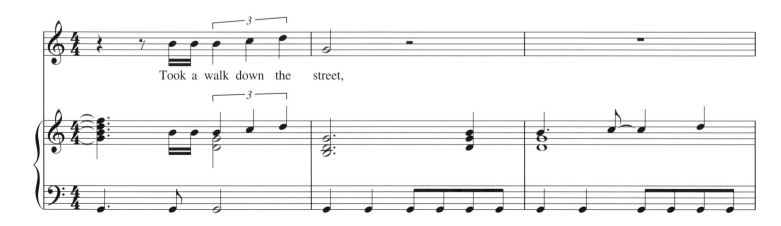

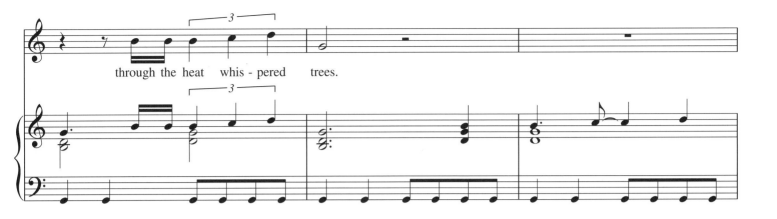

through the heat whis-pered trees.

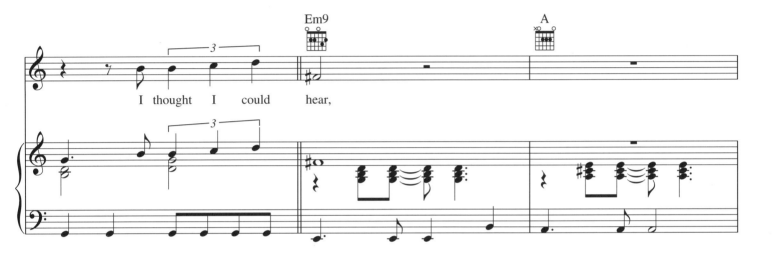

I thought I could hear,

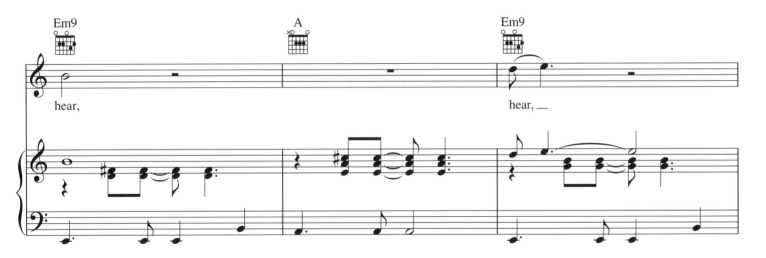

hear, hear, ___

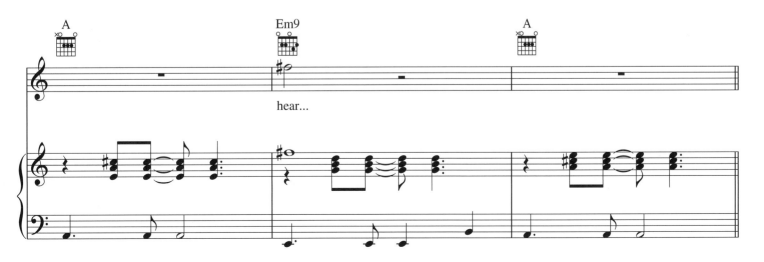

hear...

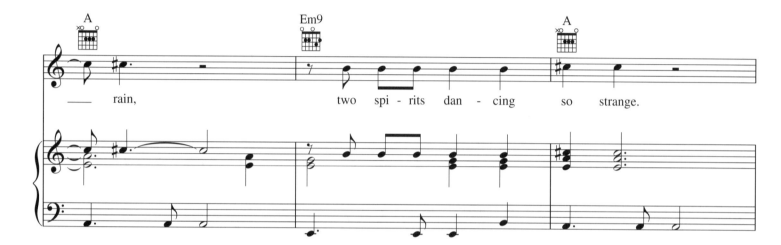

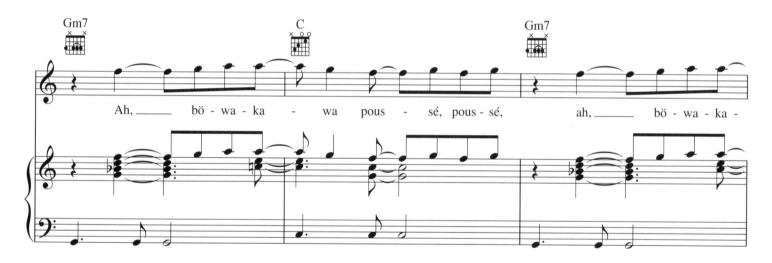

D.S. al Coda

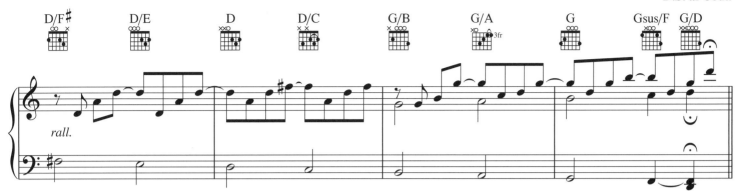

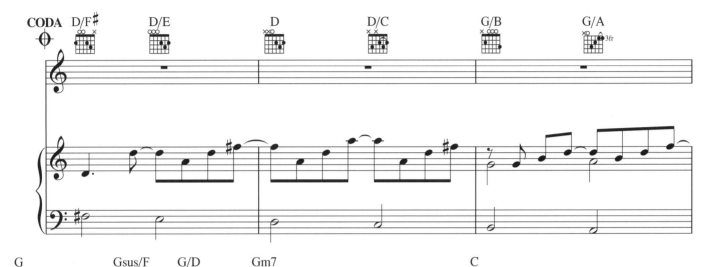

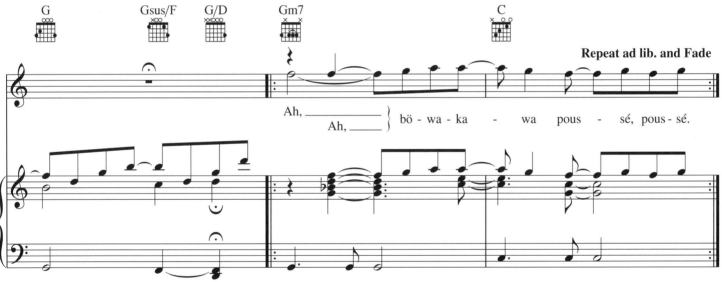

Ah, _____ } bö - wa - ka - wa pous - sé, pous - sé.
Ah, _____

**Repeat ad lib. and Fade**

*Additional Lyrics*

3. Dream, dream away
Magic in the air?
Was magic in the air?

On a river of sound
Through the mirror go round, round
I thought I could feel...
Feel... feel... feel.

4. I believe, yes I believe
More I cannot say
What more can I say?

Music touching my soul
Something warm sudden cold
The spirit dance was unfolding.

# (Just Like)
# STARTING OVER

Words and Music by
JOHN LENNON

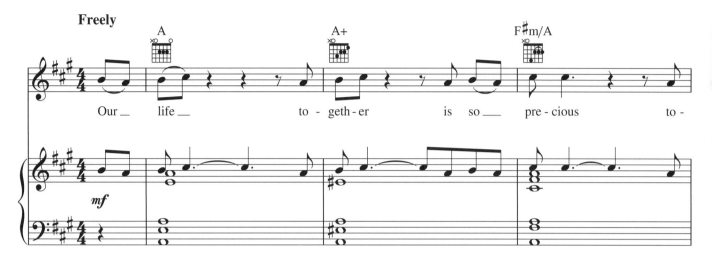

Freely

Our __ life __ to - geth - er is so __ pre - cious to-

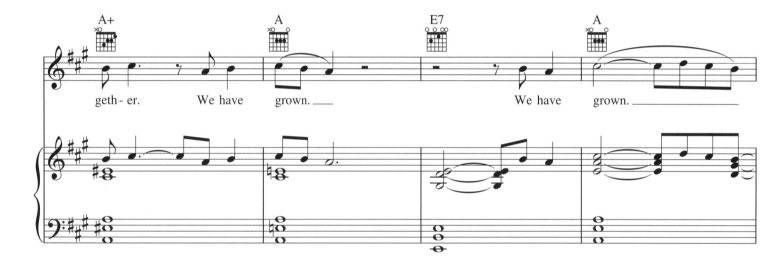

geth - er. We have grown. __ We have grown. _____

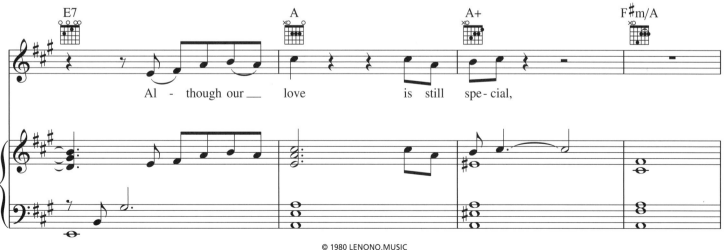

Al - though our __ love is still spe - cial,

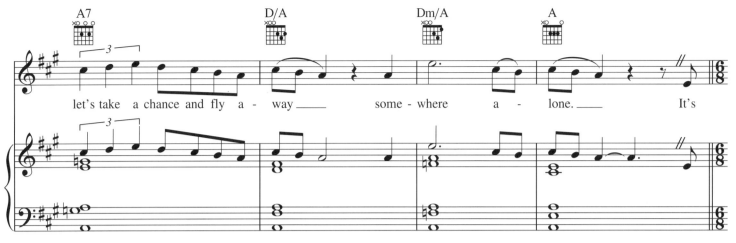

let's take a chance and fly a - way _____ some - where a - lone. _____ It's

**Moderately, with a strong beat**

been too long since we took the time. _ No ones's to blame. I know time flies _ so
day we used _ to make it, love. _ Why can't we be mak - in' love nice and

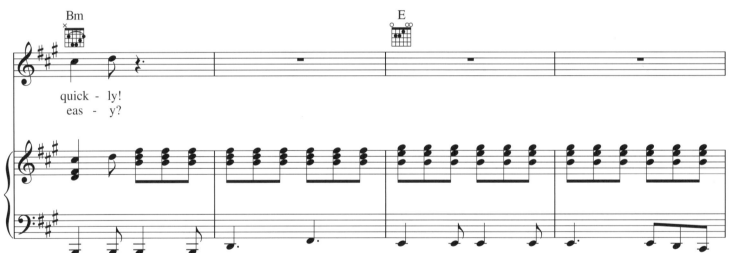

quick - ly!
eas - y?

But when I see you, dar - lin',
It's time to spread our wings and

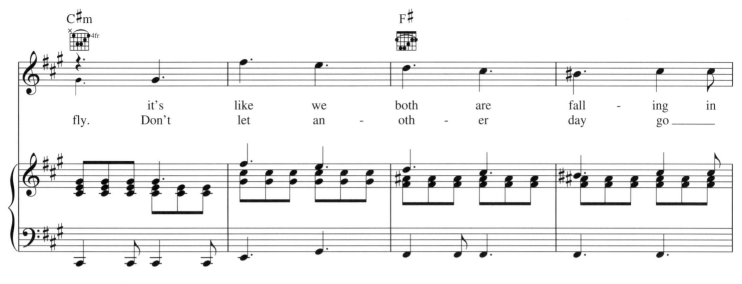

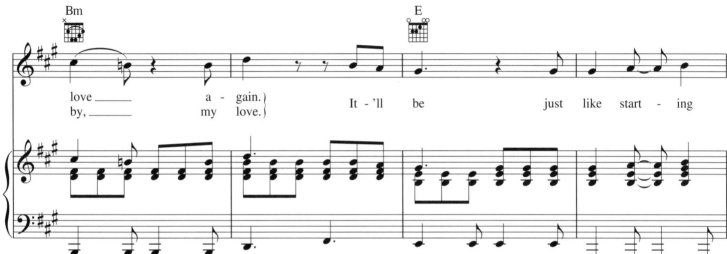

Why don't we take off a -

lone, ___                            take a trip some-where far,

far a - way. ___                We'll be to - geth - er all a -

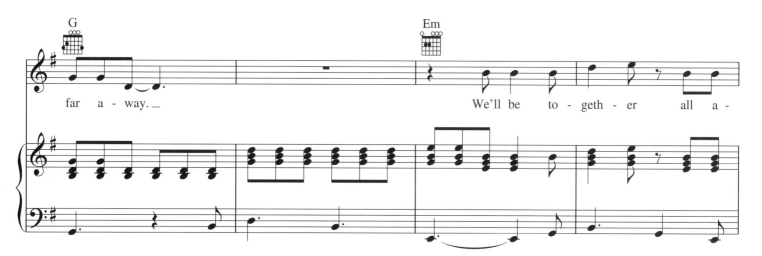

lone _____ a - gain,            like we used to ___ in the

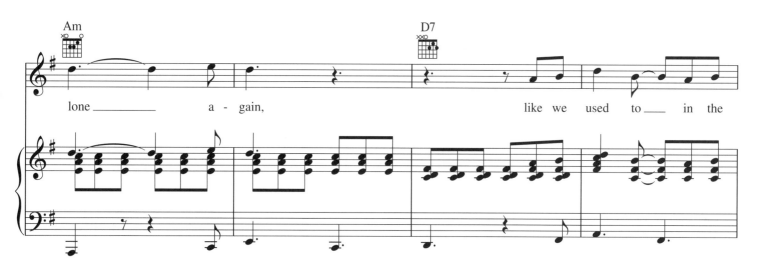

D.S. al Coda
(Verse 1)

ear - ly days. ___ Well, well, dar - lin'. It's

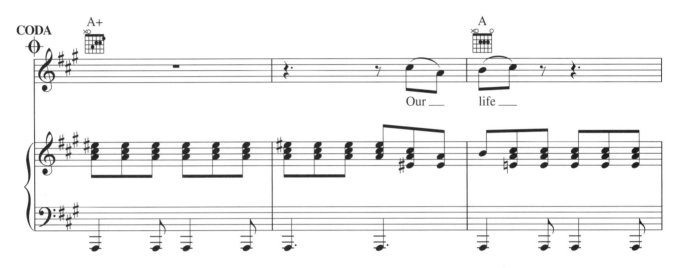

**CODA**

Our ___ life ___

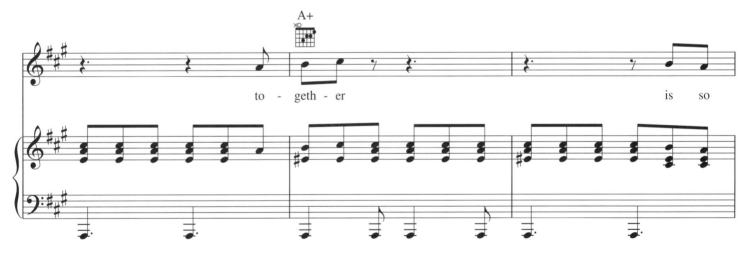

to - geth - er is so

pre - cious to - geth - er.

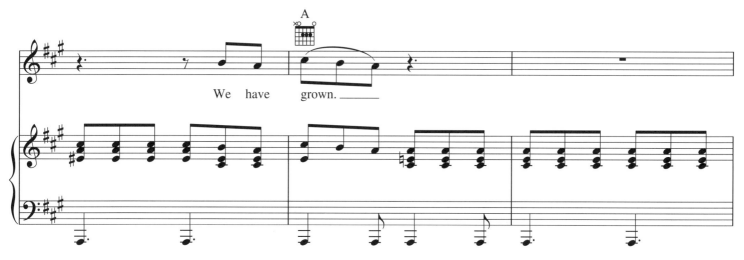

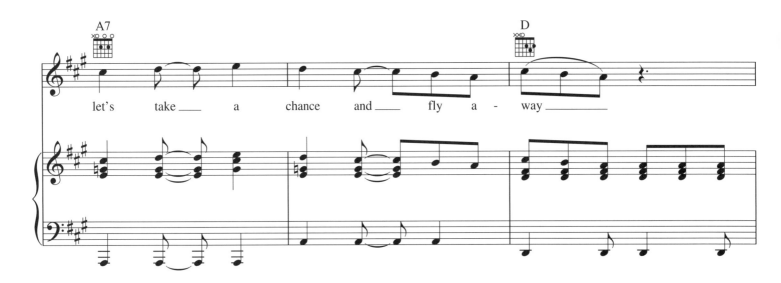

let's take ___ a chance and ___ fly a - way ___

some - where. ___

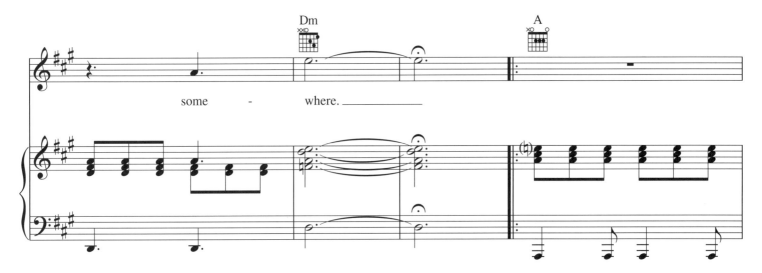

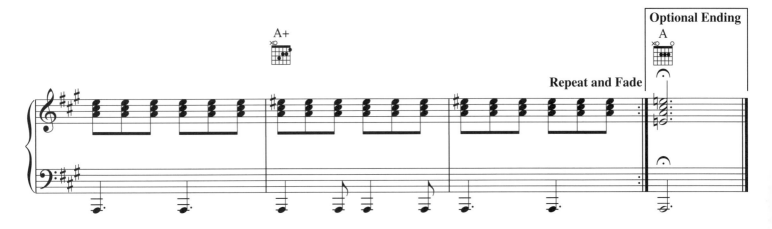

**Optional Ending**

**Repeat and Fade**

# MIND GAMES

Words and Music by
JOHN LENNON

mind games for - ev - er, ___ some kind-a dru - id dudes ___ lift-ing the veil, ___

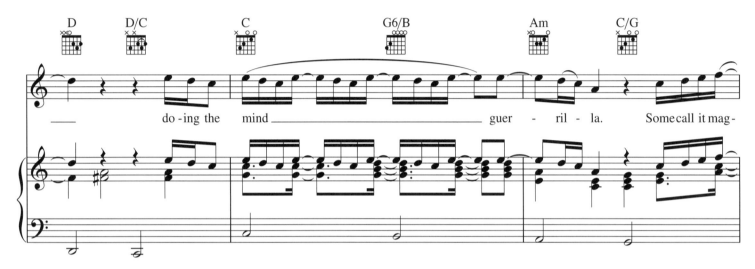

___ do-ing the mind _____ guer - ril - la. Some call it mag-

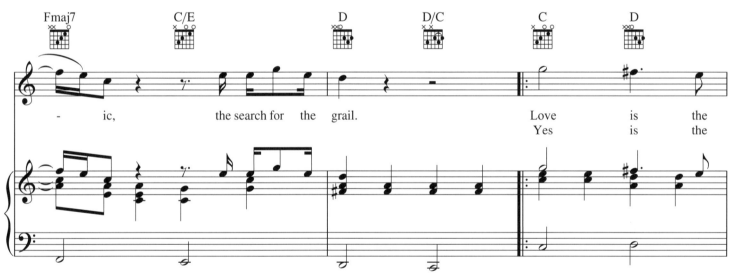

- ic, _____ the search for the grail. Love is the
Yes is the

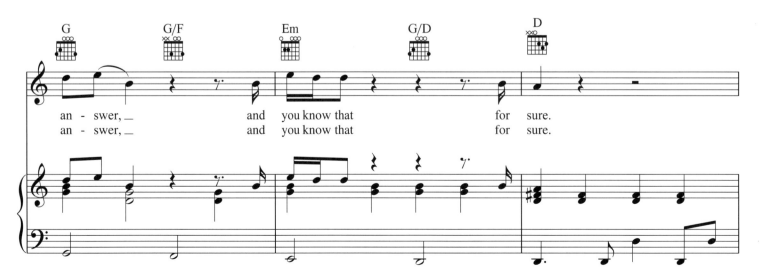

an - swer, ___ and you know that for sure.
an - swer, ___ and you know that for sure.

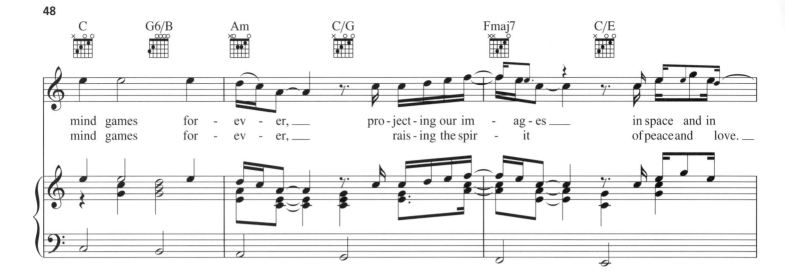

mind games for - ev - er, ___ pro - ject - ing our im - ag - es ___ in space and in

mind games for - ev - er, ___ rais - ing the spir - it of peace and love. ___

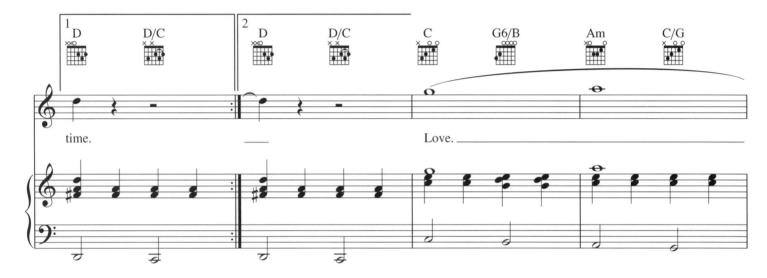

time. ___ Love. ___

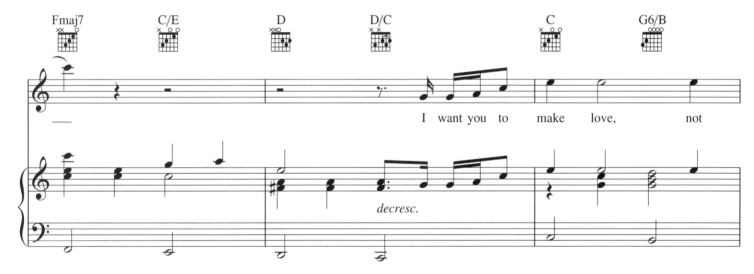

I want you to make love, not

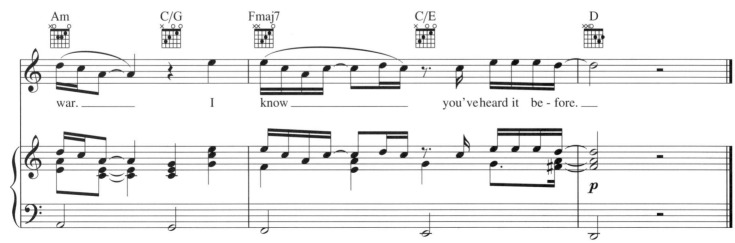

war. ___ I know ___ you've heard it be - fore. ___

# WATCHING THE WHEELS

Words and Music by
JOHN LENNON

Peo - ple say I'm cra - zy
Peo - ple say I'm la - zy,
Peo - ple ask - ing ques - tions,

do - in' what I'm do - in'. __
dream - in' my life __ a - way. __
lost in con - fu - sion. __

Well, they give me all kinds __ of warn -
Well, they give me all kinds __ of ad -
Well, I tell them there's __ no prob -

-ings ... to save me from
-vice ... de - signed to en -
-lem, ... on - ly so -

ru - in. ___ When I
light - en me. ___
lu - tions. ___ Well, they

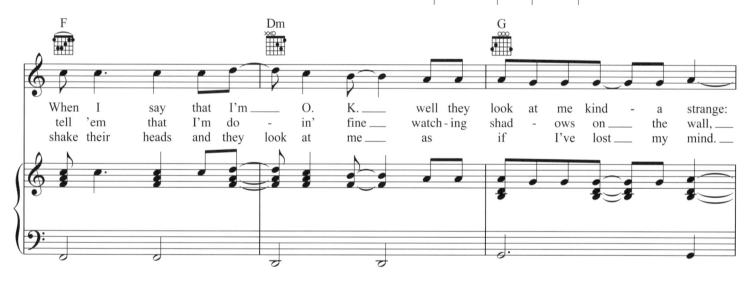

When I say that I'm ___ O. K. ___ well they look at me kind - a strange:
tell 'em say that I'm do - in' fine ___ watch-ing shad - ows on ___ the wall, ___
shake their heads and they look at me ___ as if I've lost ___ my mind.

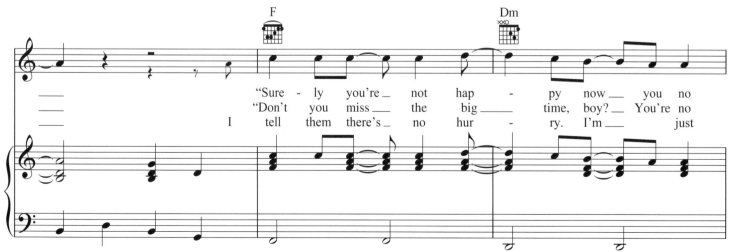

___ "Sure - ly you're ___ not hap - py now ___ you no
___ "Don't you miss ___ the big ___ time, boy? ___ You're no
___ I tell them there's ___ no hur - ry. I'm ___ just

long - er play __ the game." ____
long - er on __ the ball." _
sit - ting here do - ing time. _

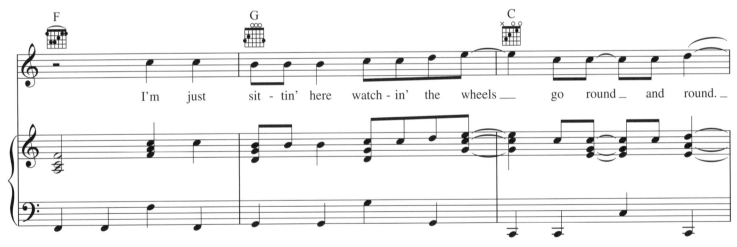

I'm just sit - tin' here watch - in' the wheels __ go round __ and round. _

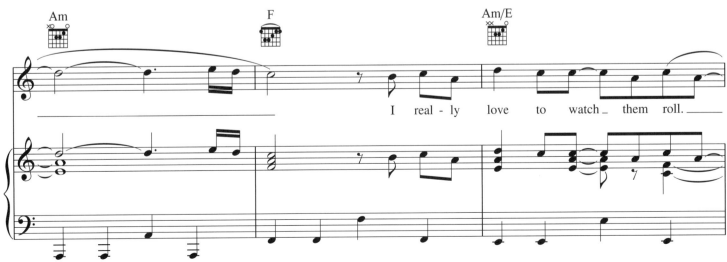

I real - ly love to watch __ them roll. ____

No long-er rid - ing on the mer - ry - go - round. _____

I just had ___ to let it go. ___

To Coda ⊕

R.H.

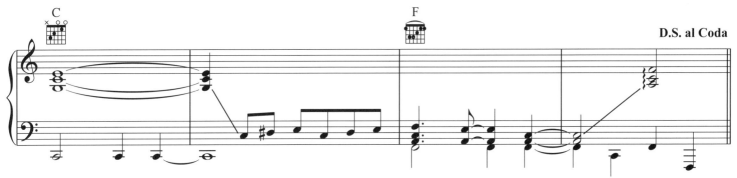

D.S. al Coda

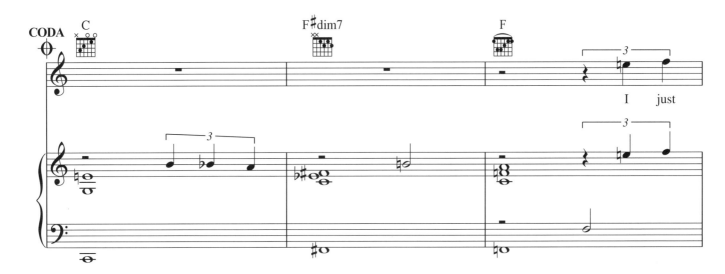

CODA

I just

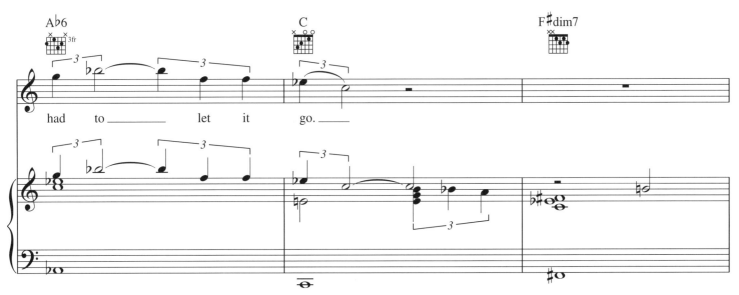

had to _____ let it go. _____

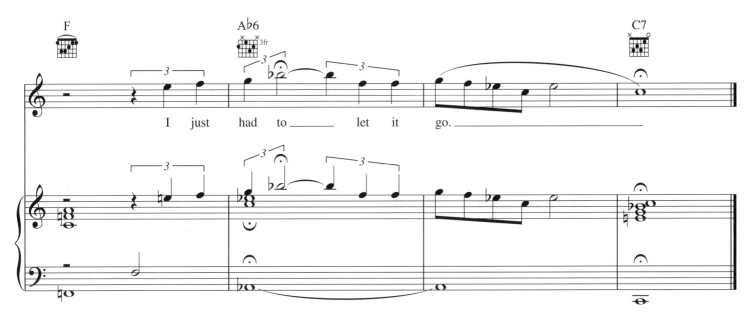

I just had to _____ let it go. _____

# STAND BY ME

Words and Music by JERRY LEIBER,
MIKE STOLLER and BEN E. KING

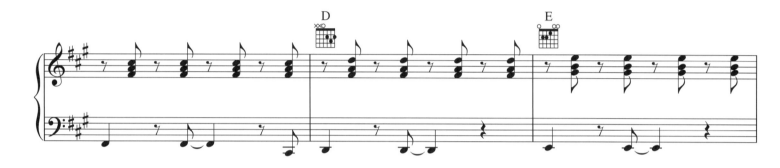

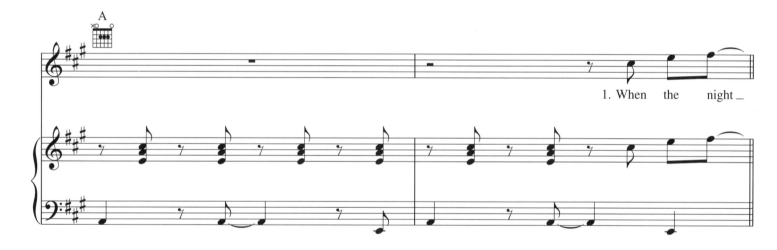

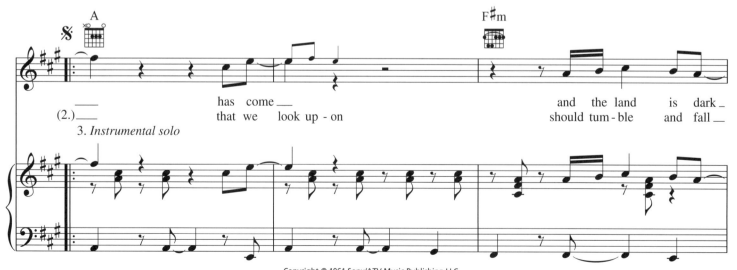

and the moon _____ is the
and the moun - tain. _____ should

on - ly light we'll see. No I won't _____
crum - ble to the sea. I won't cry, _____

be a - fraid _____ no I _____
I won't cry, _____ no I _____

won't be a - fraid _____ just as long _____ as you stand _____
won't shed a tear _____ just as long _____ as you stand _____

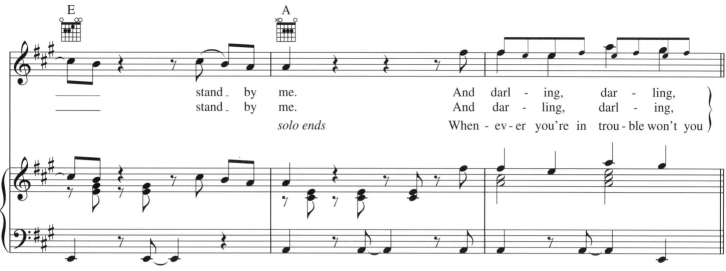

stand by me. And darl - ing, dar - ling,
stand by me. And dar - ling, dar - ling,
*solo ends* When - ev - er you're in trou - ble won't you

(1.,2.) stand by me, oh now, now, stand by
(3.) *Lead vocal ad lib.*

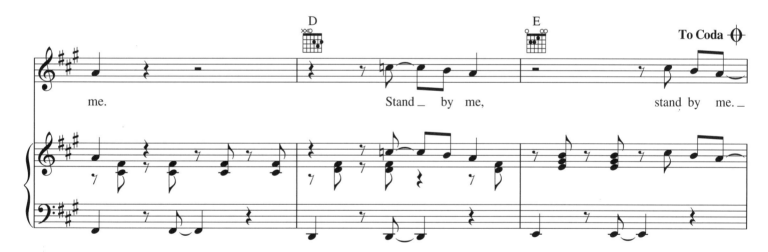

me. Stand by me, stand by me.

**To Coda** ⊕

**D.S. al Coda**

me.

2. If the sky

**CODA**

And dar - ling dar - ling

stand                by                me,                oh ____ now,                now, __

__ stand ____ by me.

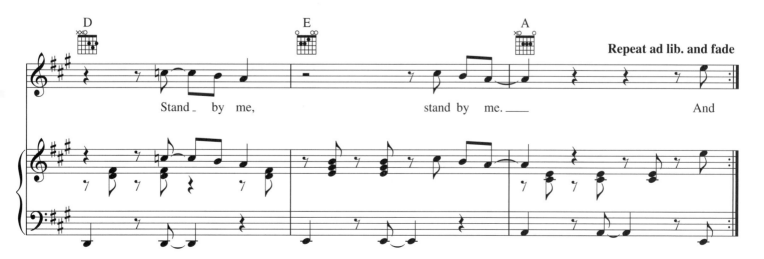

**Repeat ad lib. and fade**

Stand _ by me,                stand by me. ____                And

# IMAGINE

Words and Music by
JOHN LENNON

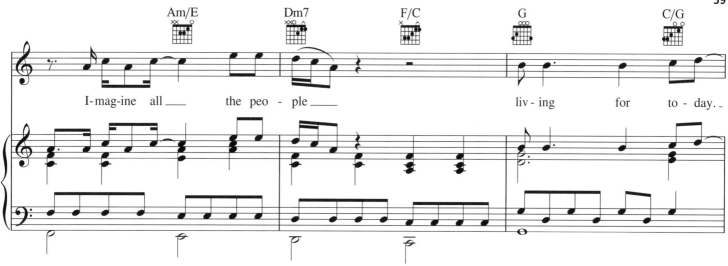

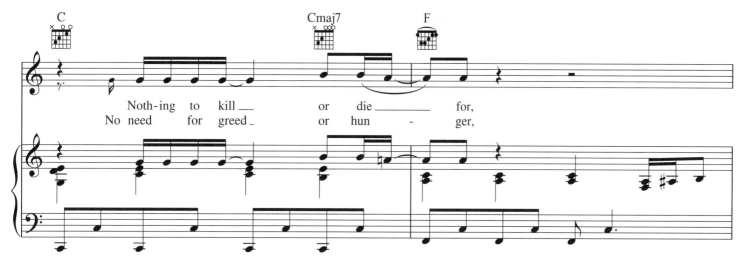

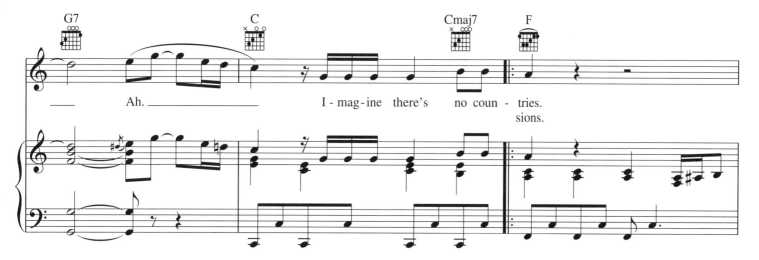

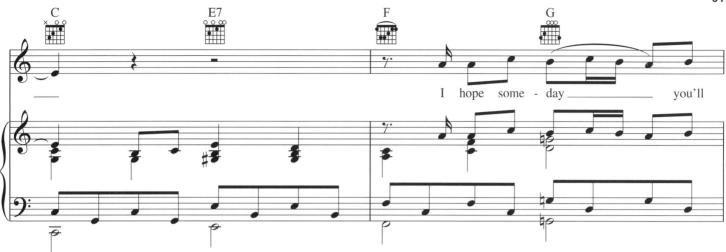

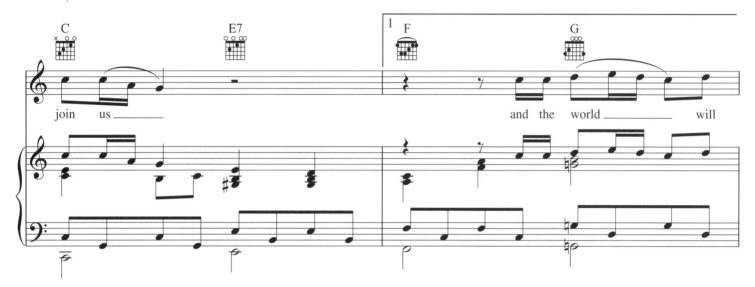

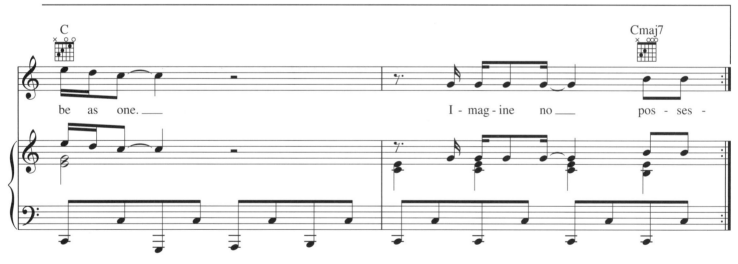

# HAPPY XMAS
## (War Is Over)

Words and Music by JOHN LENNON
and YOKO ONO

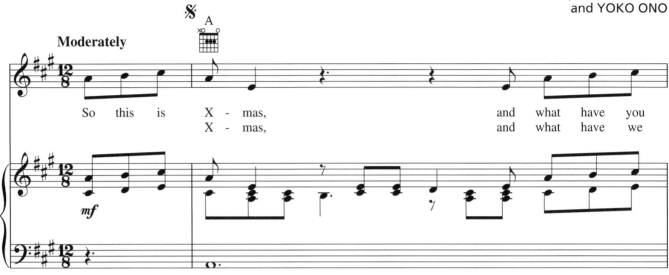

So this is X - mas,  and what have you
X - mas,  and what have we

done?  An - oth - er year o - ver,  a new one just be -
done?  An - oth - er year o - ver,  a new one just be -

gun. _____  And so this is X - mas;  I hope you have
gun. _____  And so hap - py X - mas;  we hope you have

Year. Let's hope it's a good one _____ with-out an-y

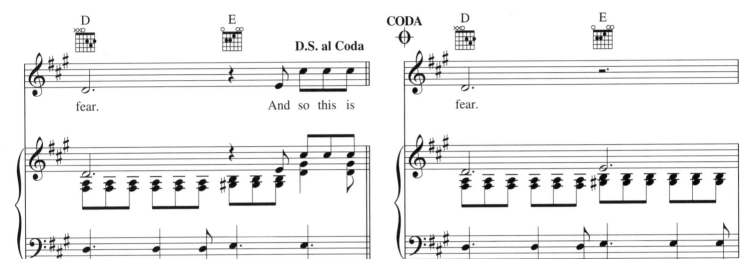

fear. And so this is **CODA** fear.

**D.S. al Coda**

War is o - ver if you want it;

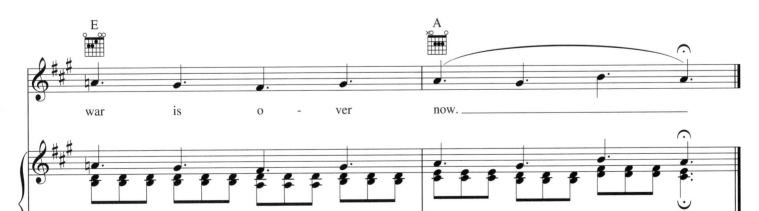

war is o - ver now. _____

# GIVE PEACE A CHANCE

Words and Music by
JOHN LENNON

Is - n't it the most?
Bye - bye Bye - byes.
Con - grat - u - la - tions.
Al - len Gins - berg, Ha - re Krish - na Ha - re, Ha - re Krish - na,

All we ___ are

G7

say - ing _____ is give peace a

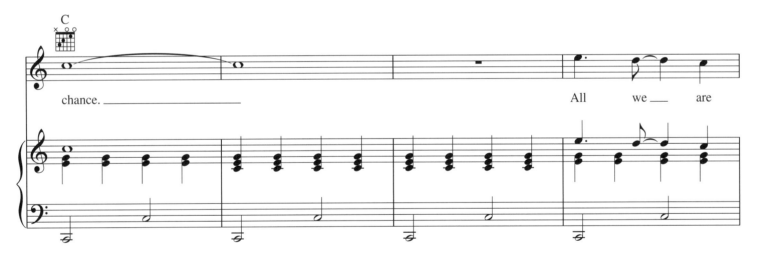

C

chance. _____ All we ___ are

G7

say - ing _____ is give peace a

chance. _____ C'- mon.

Let me tell you now. Oh, let's stick to it. All we ___ are

say - ing _____ is give peace ___ a

**Repeat ad lib. and Fade**

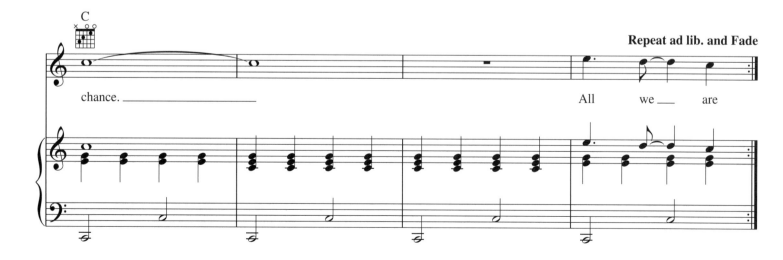

chance. _____ All we ___ are